SAINT OF THE PARTIAL APOLOGY

Copyright ©2017 Melissa Atkinson Mercer
All rights reserved. First print edition.

Five Oaks Press
Newburgh, NY 12550
five-oaks-press.com
editor@five-oaks-press.com

Cover Art: Angie Reed Garner, angiereedgarner.com

ISBN: 978-1-944355-35-7

Printed in the United States of America

SAINT OF THE PARTIAL APOLOGY

MELISSA ATKINSON MERCER

Five Oaks Press
FIVE-OAKS-PRESS.COM

Acknowledgements

About Place Journal: "Leviathan (I birthed)," "Leviathan (I'm a worry doll)," and "Leviathan (My own mother)"

Bone Bouquet: "Land of our birth" and "You fall asleep in women's houses"

Concis (Editor's Choice Award, 2016 Pith of Prose and Poem Contest): "Inside the medusa museum #11" (published as "we know how it is with windows")

Crab Fat Magazine: "Neither do I speak when I should" and "Darling, if I had to guess"

Red Paint Hill Journal: "Inside the medusa museum #1"

Storm Cellar: "Please say something different"

Sugared Water, Bramble and Thorn Anthology: "Inside the medusa museum #18"

The Fem: "Here we are in our very own lives"

White Stag, Neogoddesses: "Where you journey, they await," "They tried and tried," and "At first I was river, I was witch"

Storm Was Her Voice (dancing girl press, 2016): "Instructions for a paper earth," "In the room we come back to," "I have brought you the careful ask," "Witch creek," "Our grandmother, the mountain," "Year of no words," "Now we go quickly," "Let us speak our stories while we still can," "Sweet pilgrim," and "In the dark open of our bodies loss is written"

Contents

I

Leviathan	7
Instructions for a paper earth	8
In the room we come back to	9
At first I was river, I was witch	10
I am epistolary	11
Leviathan	12
I have brought you the careful ask	13
Witch creek	14
Our grandmother, the mountain	15
Year of no words	16
Leviathan	17
Now we go quickly	18

II

Land of our birth	19
You fall asleep in women's houses	20
Where you journey, they await	21
A man shall cleave	22
You want to give me the wrong name	23
Land of seven floods	24
They tried and tried	25
Where you are denied, I will enter	26

III

Inside the medusa museum   27

IV

Leviathan	45
[even now she is a scattering of sheep]	46
Here we are in our very own lives	47
[she is]	48
Sweet pilgrim	49
[suddenly at last]	50
Darling, if I had to guess	51
[oh the voices]	52
The maternal saint of need	53
[she is the face in the mirror]	54
Leviathan	55
[how does she manage every hour]	56
Neither do I speak when I should	57
[she enters her mirror]	58
Leviathan	59
[she is my ashes scattered there]	60
Please say something different	61
[the flowers in armloads from the fields]	62
In the dark open of our bodies loss is written	63
[she is sorry; she is perfect]	64
Let us speak our stories while we still can	65
[she is the box]	66

The young know nothing of work, my mother says   67
[she knows to act how a mother would act]   68
Leviathan   69

Notes

For my sister
For the women I know who live fiercely
For the women I don't know

I thought I could stand to look

into the centre of myself
and not fall in.

—Shara McCallum, from "My Mother as Narcissus"

I

Leviathan

I birthed a nest of mice
into the kitchen's wall: an orchard womb of prayer.

But they were loud, they deafened
my orchid-heart, bone of the only bone, the first hard fortune:

how with a bread knife I opened their sugared skulls. My children
will die and my children's children, starved for warning,

knowing more than they'll say. Here I am, the whole difference
between an earth and a god,

between a rabbit and the white church of its jaw.

Instructions for a paper earth

I carve lit ships from my bones; my fingers glimmer down to their wax.

Slight fires, even you doubt my truths.

I have promised to do well what I can only do slowly.

My limbs, pure startle, part like orchids in the black rain.

Even grief comes second-hand: dreaming a fish-skinned wolf,

dreaming a door in the rocks. Origami of the body as mother—

in one life, prophet; in one life, thief.

In the room we come back to

If nothing else, heed this: there is only one way through.

So our mother sewed us maps from the feet of wolves.
Only one voice—so she fed us tongues.

Little oracle, you too return to someone else's earth.
No one can have again the old answers.

At night, we lie down in the linens
in the press of the abandoned. Rabbits we have never known

hurl themselves against our throats' glass moon, asking
for a little more time,

a deeper light by which to burrow.

At first I was river, I was witch

So my veins bloomed with cornflowers. So my heart valve hummed with fish.
So my mother carved my lungs from sainted stone, carved me woken
and mewling, birthed me from the drainpipe
where the wild dogs slept in their hurried nests. Incessant,
she tied all my bones with phone cord and her own hair.
The more she loved me, the more she sewed
me into gowns of sea-rock and shame. My hips scrubbed hard with lye.
My lilied legs opened and I walked.

I am epistolary:

voltaic: walking the stairs of the trickster's throat: the warm green
lightening of a bullfrog's pulse.

Start again? That's all I'm ever doing:

walking again to meet you at the candle of a fox's lung:
the storms that crawl like relics from our hands.

I'm here again at the pilgrim's dress: your passageway: your dense alliterative heart:
where you promise we will

find again what we already have.

Leviathan

Probably I meant what I said. After all,
I'm a wilderness, a wolf's rotted jaw, the last day of the decade of desire.

So you see now how I cling to you:

surgical: a true ghost:
desperate for what rivers through me.

I have brought you the careful ask

Grim riot, I have scrubbed clean my face with you.

I have folded you, warm clasp, with the linens, with the sugar crusts, with the throat of a frog.

Grim racket, grim snarl—the whole world at once

would not stay in the salt-caves of me—
I was evacuated. I was run through

with greed: pressed in the pear leaves in the girth of a cow. Mother, how could rage prepare me?

I had sewn the earth like a bead in my dress; my mouth had gathered foxes like teeth.

If this room is not an ocean, tell me quickly. Surely I'd have known if my feet had ever taken to ground.

Witch creek

We grow heavy with birds: they swim our veins, they sing our throats.

We are vessel, not truth.

Bird-born liar, what mercy have I known but you?

Dusk climbs shimmer-toothed from the water, deep blue bone. Any body but mine could be the way out; believe me, I've considered it.

Our nightgowns walk, half-limbed and somber, in the garden of lotus candles.

We could let them speak. There is no terror greater than another.

Our grandmother, the mountain,

went mad, our mother told us, tried to burn the kitchen table—fire to drown water, to kill the sea-scent in her clothes. She filled the creek with birds, but they swam, quick-scaled and writhing. Cruel sinner, what woman does not want the earth she has forged? And yet, dear ghost, tell no one: I, too, know the simple heart—we all lose what we cannot carry. Like you, I know now what I may not later. Like you, I grow weary, neck-deep in the river garden, fish faces like lanterns turning to me by the thousands.

Year of no words

The base of my throat where I touch it each hour: loose, like a lantern
carried to a field of small stones. I'm amazed by what's required—
geese moving through the damp morning, north over the creek-bed.
You say you've seen hills change into birds and join them. I, too,
have seen rage. I, too, know to count the earth daily:
pinning the wet sheets above my head, each one
tender like the inside of a farm animal's ear.
What I have said before, even you cannot tell me. Even I
have not heeded, though I heard
my voice quick after me
like a fox.

Leviathan

I walk into a dream, a hot white sea, the crypt of the honeycombed heart:
into a constellation of lungs:

(I'm a lost book, a confrontation):

into a porcelain dusk that watches from beneath the sugar moon,
the fish mirror, the lotus soap I spent all day making.

Being where you are is one way of trying: (a lighthouse scaffolding

the moon over the shore): but hardly the best way, as I'm sure
you're learning by now.

Now we go quickly

Animals fly from the trucks the neighbor boys race down the black gravel:
seabirds, lizards, moths: two by two by thousands

rioting into the fruit fields. So we take in their salt-blue eggs,
hatch them in our dishwater, in our fire-pots, on the tops of our feet.

What we have made we keep making. Tell me, is there anything
the heart-water will not curl around like a rock?

They are moaning in our throats; they are wearing our dresses.
Clever, cavernous thieves—

we give and give until our hands bleed ships.

II

Land of our birth

Say again how great men walk on water, salt glimmered, on the backs of fish-haired women. Say duplicity. Say your mother had a baby and it's you, it's temptation. Say you drank apple milk from her hands, that she stitched the high tide to your foot, her voice to your teeth. Say a hundred mothers, feeding the wailing young. Say insatiable. Little singe, little prophet, your limbs grew firm with their songs. You emptied their throats of sound.

You fall asleep in women's houses

You touch them and dream, singe-mongered, your own stabbing: blue jeweled knife, water from the kitchen sink. Metal rabbits, lungs predicting like clocks. Your mother's tongue in a pearl box. Doors in the river, doors in the rocks. A woman's bones. Too dark to know if they are fish, if they are this world or the next. Sugared breath in the stiff sheets. You dream her wrong-limbed and shimmer; cruel listen.

Where you journey, they await

You said *let me be homeless* so you were, so our mothers welcomed you, washed your throat with honey blossom, hewed you a chair from their teeth. Herald of the land of surrender, you are riding the backs of glass cattle. You are shattering clocks with their hoofs. Though you erase our mothers, though they no longer open their gills to breathe, do not grow boastful; when the floods come, they will tilt up their faces and swim.

A man shall cleave

Oh, women are wicked, my new mother said. *Don't hurry, don't hurry,* said my first. I was sweet dark—apple thicket veined with fog—while you knocked at doors that didn't hold me, waited, fire-ready, to guide me to my lover's bed. Prophet, harken: send the little mob home. Yes, I am giver; I will be with you one lantern. I will carry you ghost, ghost to the flood road.

You want to give me the wrong name

When I ask for my mother's, you hand me the door to the cellar: sweet rot of pig head, cow shoulder. I ask, clever specter, to stitch one, but you chop the ribbons with a steak knife, you feed the lace to mules. At night now my limbs go blank as windows. Bold as summon. I stack clean the bowls in the cupboard. I lift my tongue and clamor.

Land of seven floods

Windows open out to a sea that slopes away, green and tight. *So many words mean wait*, my mother says, loosening her knife in the fruit field. Light catches in the hills and holds while the rest of the town darkens. A red-doored church grows evening from its heart; in every world, women are closing their lives.

They tried and tried

Pink-shelled trees. Mountains splintering in damp light. The town bridge wailing, woven from the hair of the girl who lost her way, following otters into river, changing bone for sand, breath for rock. Not bride, not daughter. No sound could call her. Small oracle in the church of the nameless where we sit now and gather, where we touch the moon to our pilgrim ears.

Where you are denied, I will enter

Dusk in the road of weeping cherries where I sing bees to sleep under the nettle, where I gather them in my ears; I take them as my tongue. Ready, writhing sin. You have said the earth is built from the voice of men, the heart of women. You have asked for love without words. Strange prophet, I will shriek in the salt-caves. I will knock at the hills until they open, until my bones are wolves.

III

Inside the medusa museum

#1

we know beauty passes//and it did

winged horses shuddering in my soon-severed throat

but wait//back up

start with
mother hated light//would stand
in the wet black//ladling soup into the bowl//of the calf's only head

[why even tell this story]

start with
father would not speak on holy days//held a candle in the knock
beneath his tongue

[because it's mine and no one//will let me have it]

#2

gods walk through me like a plague of locusts

as in hag
fishwife//gorgon//witch

as in battle-ax
did anyone say we could be here//anyone at all

as in

if mother says no//ask father
if the beasts say no//ask the dolls

#3

a miracle girl on her knees in the mud
[an apple heat//a black orchid]

and I want it//the immensity of asking

but my tongues are snails//come up hungered
as old candles in a long room

the cows too on their knees in the marigolds
[the savaged yellow of my bone wanting out]

I a rabbit in your pilgrim's dress//a pilgrim scraping//sugar from a blackened pot

welcome to the punctual famine
the immediate lust//the first

dear syllable of need

#4

a dead calf caught in the muddy reeds
in the same river we drink from
[why//you know why]

the orchards witch-dark
loosened into miracles
[I want to confound you//make you try//a little harder]

the same calf that stumbled in the alleyway of the valve I carry
come//paint keys on our feet//saints on our doors

dear mother in the stairs of my throat
what will you do when you have no words

[yes someone knows the way//but it is not//me]

#5

let's say I'm hungry
let's say I cannot speak

that my knuckles are the teeth of new birds//warm and blind in a mother's nest
that my knees are the tongues of badgers

let's say I deal in miracles

that you know//what happens next

#6

I sleep beneath wildebeests
humming in the tall grass

I sleep in the anthem of a stranger's body

[yes you confuse me
for someone else//someone who also
is not yours]

I say who's there and you say who's looking
I say are you sure//are you entire/intoxicating//are you digging in the
     apple roots/in the black orchid
are you still hungry

while geese murmur from the fog like a voice from a body

[my body//the whole body] their hearts glistened
under a dark and certain flight

#7

too late//I've named my monsters
the named thing can walk right in//it can inhabit

meet doubt//guiding my heart like a kite through bone
meet false fortune//charming the bison to my rivered lungs

welcome water breather//welcome rib
caged with paper dolls
formed from my newest tongue//confusion

of noun//of purpose and cause//dear autopsy [dear former truth]

I ask nothing from you//the monsters

humming in my spine's open mile
the cornfields whispering to the velvet black

#8

let's say I entered the temple//what now

let's say I wore the hand of a god like a pilgrim's woven dress//but why
    say anything

let's say I was proud in the country of my long bone
a long history of women//madly in love//with the way things weren't

there//that's better//that's the best

way I know to tell you
pity crawled beside me like a wet fox//braiding its fur through my breath

for all at once//I was hideous//prone
to the violence of others

memory flew from me like a colorless bird

#9 [in which men imagine my death]

and then I could guess//the dreams of others

as I//ossuary//under the scarves we laid to dry
in the olive heat

stars melting into wide leaves//into my anger's deep root

[dear bone room//equal parts what I loved and what I wanted//to love

while you spoke for a cause
to which you had made//no sacrifice]//yes I knew then//the dream

of another and it took me//from myself
like the first ice//the battlepath//of the fish beneath

while my demon hands kept tending//the honeybees//my demons

blooming like marigolds with the poison
I boiled in my mother's//iron pots

#10 [in which men begin their quests]

do I know your name
have I buried you

once but not twice//twice but not enough
if you're coming//are you coming now

the wolves of my mortality announce me
one of us a howl of moon//one of us a desperate path

many times father said no one
would find the mark he left on this earth//but I did

and I've been there//I've held whole
countries on my ceaseless tongue

#11

we know how it is with windows//how that night

mother opened them and slept
heard girls singing//to each other in the olive trees

heard her own lung//gnawing its way through rib

crawling along the blue walls//out into the miracle
of the night's only wolf//and waking

how she could only//breathe half the air//speak

half the words she knew//a beast born to beasts
into a morning black and hot as a rabbit's womb

into a shirt pressed wet against her skin

#12 [in which I am mortal]

the only one who wakes to only//so many mornings

dear martyr//welcome

to the final epidemic of need
the nightmare woven//in the dusk of a rabbit's paw

welcome mother//waiting//in line to buy milk
father//waiting to welcome a god

[or]

mother//bathing in the river's milk
welcome father//sewing//lamps into the wings of a horse

darling if you have any questions//if you still//have questions

speak//speak now

and now

#13

you don't know hunger//the way I do
can't see it as it comes

dreams of sewer lines//clogged with my own//severed head

plagues of snails//eating whole
horses and cows from the throat of the pasture's dark

it must have changed me//this knowing

this shameless habit of opening doors
between the now and never//between the beasts and dolls

calves born backward from the womb//so yes

I try hardest//at all the wrong times
tattoos on my hands//tattoos on my hands and feet

a written history//of the things you'll never write

#14 [in which//yes//I will tell you my flaws]

call me an intricate guess//a dollhouse//something that can be walked into
call me the great sin//of talking of a thing as it happens

I have a mother born blind//I
was born blind//born frantic

at the success of others//a shameless apostle
one who desires stones

who grows uncertain in a grave//as my mother
rinsed in dark oil//a seed between her lips

began wailing//years
after the fact//as the orchard's black music grew//from the knock inside
    her throat

#15

there were no snakes//none//it's okay

to ask once//but this//is the seventh time

seven times we built our town on the corpses of cows
seven times we rubbed our hands with honeybees to make them bleed
seven times I stood in the immense field of longing//breaking off my
    bones to fill the muddy creeks with fish
seven times I reached for you in the hot black//under the patterned quilt
seven times I said enough//I said at least I know better//I said I dreamt
    only once//of milk snakes//but darling//they are never far

#16 [in which I am offered love [or] death]

tell me//have you figured it out

palpable//[or] predatory//only young by halves

pretty as a horse in winter
[or]
a beast can't dream even

a brave act [or] the very first lie//tell me

if I gave you what you wanted would you want it still

rabbits falling in lust in the hot rocks//reaching
toward the dark of a tree//[or]

like you I'm weary//born to suffer//in the most common ways

#17

and so I began and could not stop

at first only toads and mice
a young swan in the muddy creek//a nest of deer in the mist

they grew so peaceful//to stone//as I took their wanting

into the museum of the heart
hatchets stacked against glass

as I took from them the music//the acoustic ache

and then it was rivers//hills//the left side of the sky at night
everything stone//every wanting

washed//labeled//displayed//inside the woman

who could be a thousand women//the woman who took
every miracle she could

#18

my throat was a light so certain
mother said//she couldn't close her eyes to it

though she tried//to sleep in the long wet heat

though it called things home

foxes the color of holiness running startled from the blue hills
moths abandoning a trail of lace through the corn fields

what I meant to say//who are we to decide which life is life

[was I the key//the doll's head//the dark-jeweled consequence]
when we don't even know how to look

when my body is a wolf's cave and I say miracle

and I mean it now
though I never did then

IV

Leviathan

I'm an embryo, a sculpture of cows. Stones washed into a dirt road.

What am I working on now? I mean
what's in it for me:

a witch hunt, a flawed theology?

My ancestors were the saints of the partial apology,
the architecture of a future performance. Tell me you'd have done things differently:

(I promise it's that simple): tell me you'd have held my hand.

even now she is a scattering of sheep
grazing
under a sky

that looks down again into the brown water

she herself has failed
whatever she is

she said she'd be back soon

Here we are in our very own lives:

our cemetery of broken dolls, a whole year
of mice asleep in the black cedar.

I mean, go ahead: unmake me. I'm reasonably sure I can manage.

I've been the builder of moons from the small fish of a smaller creek,
deep fog from the words I almost said.

Humility was the name I took once, the name we shared,

before we knew how full the earth
with the things a woman must become.

she is
cemeteries browsed at night by dogs

she's the center
of something new and wild

Sweet pilgrim,

I have considered every endeavor.

I could swim the clawfoot tub to you.
I could shimmer you, wind-chimed, in the pear leaves.

Still not sacred. Still not spectacle. My feet could bleed.

I could walk the sea glass of you and be no closer.
After all, what is love if not in me, moth-winged and terrored?

I was always the wrong ask, our mother's butchered child.

Darling, be the steady soul;
a liar's road is long.

suddenly at last
the burnt-out candles like the most perfect room

much of the world has prevailed

(and if she's past help
still here

in this moment as it passes)—

Darling, if I had to guess

I'd tell you my heart valves were a set of butcher's knives,

that we each of us
must leave something behind in this earth.

My own mother was capricious: gave us fire bugs: the fury of a thousand eyes.

And her mother: the mountain:
the arthritic flower of her spine. Believe me,

what you ask now, I ask always and again: how can anyone trust the body

if we can't know what crawls
antlered from the white ash?

(oh the voices

the voices are always here
do you mind

it could be the most ordinary thing)

The maternal saint of need

Pardon me, I'm catastrophic:
the blood magic of a fish-girl's moon, the answer no one wished nor wanted.

A creature of true grit, as my mother said, shaking her head.

For years I thought this happened to everyone.
For years I was the train whistle, the tornado drill, the knife in the caved
    lungs of the god of the honey-lit river.

For years I was my own yearning ear. But, lovely, when we say *for years*,

don't we mean *now*? Don't we always
mean now?

she is the face in the mirror
the fur of animals she has killed and skinned

she is powerful a curl of crust

a girl witnessing in fury
a practiced flick of the knife

Leviathan

Bulls kneel in the sugar cane in the brown river:
while I am growing there in secret:

the fierce red-flowered rain:

while my bones become a metronome,
a line of painted bowls, a haunting

in the house of wandering saints.

*how does she manage every hour
to be so exactly*

the same

Neither do I speak when I should:

culpable, amphibious: my slug-tongue glimmered in the bloodroot,
the blue gardenias of my lungs

heavy with divination: how from cacophony I formed the embryos of wolves

inside the womb of the forbidden wood
of my mouth's only prophet.

No one said to me, *come.* No one said, *use what you have.*

No one said, *when we asked for you—truly, lovely—*
this was what we most desired.

she enters her mirror just as she's always been

her ship her green coastline where bees hum among the grapes

*(darling I tell you I'm enchanted
ecstatic to see you*

at the hour you were actually expected)

Leviathan

I'm a worry doll, a wish, a museum of hatchets:

the circus of the easy answer. I'm the cow chased from the road
by a boy in an unwashed robe,

the same boy who tied back my hair with daises, who prayed to my dark bones

as they coffined in the moon of our harvest: the boy
who sits with us now in the apple grove

braiding long strands of bread. Don't worry, love, it's only a feast

for the witches, the saints we have burned
and burned again.

she is my ashes scattered there

a high dune in the summer
indestructibly furious (I hardly

had any trouble finding her)

Please say something different

If it happened: the wilderness of memory, the knife, the baptismal fossil. If my mother

escaped the midnight war, the milk moon of her pale and bloody feet.

If everyone was so lucky.
If I'm a star carved from a fish's lung, from the core of a fallen apple.

If I prove myself real. Lovely, if I cannot

begin this fight again.

the flowers in armloads from the fields
as if in prayer

the minor goddess of those who enter
standing shyly in a vestibule

where did she get such presence

she's still a girl
a dark nervous hour

In the dark open of our bodies loss is written

Trees kneel in the low, early light. You take such care breaking

their roots from your legs as you move toward the kitchen window.

Except I can never recall you—not perfectly, not even now:

blurred line of your shoulders along the blue houses, thick grass woven with birds.

Already I am letting the world have itself as it wants.

And you walk, you always walk

out of a fog pinned up around you like faded sheets. And your face—a vast stone room,

the high-arching turret of your bone—

she is sorry; she is perfect (did you make a wish too)

Let us speak our stories while we still can

For weeks, the river, swollen snarl, runs through rocks like a wolf
while we knead salt-bread under the kitchen's bulb
and rub new kittens with warm cloths:
small heretics, born to an earth so wrong
that their limbs must scale, their sides gather breath.

More and more lately, I can only guess at my life.

Of course there's no voice but the loudest voice; the whole earth's been telling me.

In the lit-root gorge, cows wail and shriek. They know so many words.
They burn their feet on stars.

she is the box in which she keeps her failures

the extravagant wrong the sweater worn once
probably
right now

***The young know nothing of work,* my mother says**

Beyond us, the garden is a small cup of light, gathering from the kitchen.

I love the way your hands become my hands, a trick of shadow.

Mother, forgive us. Our words break the sky into mountains.

Last week's storm shook the clotheslines loose;

I imagined the wind—part of my body's body. Believe me, I understand

that we are the sieve through which the years move.

All summer, we hated the tree collards, their arching spines.

But isn't it beautiful how they turn and pull, like tongues in a new blue earth?

she knows to act how a mother would act

can't help thinking of now
as the past
a bird flown in through the flowers

but first

if you pass through the wrong door
right here

on this corner—

Leviathan

My own mother gave me the year of my journey,
the fish-girl in my shattered lung.

Does it start there: my passion for the project of my life:

where every place I left became a sea, a flood village,
a warning light in the hill of wolves:

the dry rotted caves of their teeth where the people waited

for my death, where they stretched snake skins into drums,
where they sang for me: my first and only praise.

Notes

The italicized sequence in Section IV is a found poem. Source material: Cunningham, Michael. *The Hours.* Picador, 1998.

[even now she is a scattering of sheep]: pages 3-5
[she is]: pages 49-51
[suddenly at last]: pages 41-42
[oh the voices]: page 198
[she is the face in the mirror]: pages 85-86
[how does she manage every hour]: 84
[she enters her mirror]: page 114
[she is my ashes scattered there]: pages 131-132
[the flowers in armloads from the fields]: pages 217-219
[she is sorry; she is perfect]: page 206
[she is the box]: page 181
[she knows to act how a mother would act]: pages 47-51

More Titles from Five Oaks Press:

Drugstore Blue, by Susan H. Case
Model Organism, by Robert Pesich
Spectators, by Rob Davidson
One Throne, by Rae Hoffman Jager
Hooked Through, by Sara Wagner

About the Author

Melissa Atkinson Mercer is the author of five poetry chapbooks, including *Star-Blind in the Family of Fortune Keepers* (Hermeneutic Chaos Press), *After the Miracle Season* (Seven Kitchens Press), and *ghost exhibit* (Glass Poetry Press). Her work has been selected to appear in *Zone 3*, *Bone Bouquet*, *Blue Earth Review*, *Ruminate*, and *Fiolet & Wing: an Anthology of Domestic Fabulism,* among others, and has been nominated for Best of the Net and a Pushcart Prize. She has an MFA from West Virginia University, where she won the Russell MacDonald Creative Writing Award in Poetry.

www.ingramcontent.com/pod-product-compliance
Lightning Source LLC
Chambersburg PA
CBHW071748080526
44588CB00013B/2183